E

03

Henry Priestley, 1953.

THE RAILWAY PHOTOGRAPHY
OF HENRY PRIESTLEY

COLIN GARRATT

SUTTON PUBLISHING

First published in 2000 by
Sutton Publishing Limited · Phoenix Mill
Thrupp · Stroud · Gloucestershire · GL5 2BU

British Library Cataloguing in Publication Data
A catalogue record for this book is available from the British Library.

ISBN 0-7509-2508-6

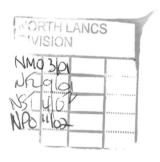
Typeset in 10/12 pt Palatino.
Typesetting and origination by
Sutton Publishing Limited.
Printed and bound in England by
J.H. Haynes & Co. Ltd, Sparkford.

Contents

Abbreviations

For historical and geographical reasons, railway names are given as existing in pre-Grouping days and use the following abbreviations. Also included are the pre-Nationalisation railways – the 'Big Four'.

BMR	Brecon & Merthyr Railway
BR	Barry Railway (also British Railways)
CLC	Cheshire Lines Committee
CR	Caledonian Railway
FR	Furness Railway
GCR	Great Central Railway
GER	Great Eastern Railway
GNR	Great Northern Railway
GNR(I)	Great Northern Railway of Ireland
GS&WR	Great Southern & Western Railway
GWR	Great Western Railway
HR	Highland Railway
LBSCR	London, Brighton & South Coast Railway
LDECR	Lancashire, Derbyshire & East Coast Railway
LMS	London, Midland & Scottish Railway
LNER	London & North Eastern Railway
LNWR	London & North Western Railway
LSWR	London and South Western Railway
LYR	Lancashire & Yorkshire Railway
M&GNJR	Midland & Great Northern Joint Railway
MR	Midland Railway
MS&LR	Manchester, Sheffield & Lincolnshire Railway
NBR	North British Railway
NER	North Eastern Railway
RR	Rhymney Railway
S&MJR	Stratford upon Avon & Midland Junction Railway
S&DJR	Somerset & Dorset Joint Railway
TVR	Taff Vale Railway

Introduction

A close friend of Henry Priestley once described him as an Olympian, an accolade which eloquently describes this remarkable man. Henry Benjamin Priestley was born in the reign of Edward VII; he is Britain's oldest active railway photographer and, on days when the weather is suitable, he still travels considerable distances by train to record, in colour, the face of the new railway. Priestley's photography includes two principal disciplines: rail transport and medieval architecture. He taught chemistry and physics before gaining an MA from London University and was headmaster of a grammar school from 1950 until 1975. He is also an accomplished classical organist specialising in the works of Bach, which he performs with great pleasure.

I first met Henry when my company, Milepost 92½, was publishing a book on trams in association with the National Tramway Museum at Crich. Their picture archivist, Glyn Wilton, soon convinced me that Henry Priestley's collection of tramway photographs was the finest in existence. Almost the entire collection was held at Crich. Priestley's work was so comprehensive that we were able to illustrate the entire book, covering the whole of Britain, from his negatives; selecting these gave me an unparalleled insight into his photographic style. The book, *The Golden Age of British Trams*, was a great success, and has probably never been bettered by any other pictorial work on this subject.

Before that book appeared, Priestley was not widely known as a photographer; very little of his work had been published, and I knew nothing of his railway legacy. During the production of the tram book I undertook a series of recorded interviews with him for Crich's archive and it was during one of these – in a chance remark – that I heard of his railway legacy. 'Twelve thousand negatives', he said with great composure. I couldn't get the words out fast enough, 'Where are they?' I asked. 'All sold' came the devastating reply; 'the last ones only months ago.' The collection had been sold piecemeal. The true importance of this heritage was made even more clear when Henry explained that he had been influenced by T.R. Perkins, who wrote in the early editions of *The Railway Magazine*. Perkins's aim was to travel on every railway in Britain – a formidable undertaking in the 1920s – and especially so for a practising chemist with a shop in Henley-in-Arden; and, as Henry pointed out, his free time would only have been on Saturday afternoons and Sundays and a two-week annual holiday. Priestley strove to emulate Perkins, but also using a camera, and so photographing most stations and junctions in the realm.

It became immediately obvious that the intrinsic value of Priestley's pictures lay in their collectivity; parts of a vast jigsaw which, when pieced together, would result in a national heirloom. Henry knew of no organisation that would have been prepared to buy such a collection, as Crich had done with the trams. Had we at Milepost known of the legacy, we would have intervened to keep it intact.

In the instant, I realised that Milepost should attempt to put the collection back together again and, over subsequent meetings, Henry detailed where many pictures had gone and contact was made with the individuals concerned. The response was positive; many people had bought a batch of Priestleys for certain particular pictures and were happy to pass over the remainder; in other instances we were able to exchange or purchase. Milepost now holds some 4,000 Priestleys – about a third of his output – and this book has been put together from the negatives in our possession.

In the introduction to my previous book on Henry Priestley, as part of Milepost's 'Great Railway Photographers' series, I wrote: 'there are moments when I regard Henry Priestley as the finest railway photographer of all time.' One reads his pictures as one does a page of text, noting the elegance of the composition. Priestley has an innate ability to place the salient elements into rhythmic patterns and capture beautifully the atmosphere and essence of a location – this is one of his greatest attributes. Another was his vision to cover the whole of Britain – an incredible concept considering how vast our railway network once was. In many cases he only had the opportunity to visit a location once and, accordingly, he had to work with whatever weather and other circumstances prevailed at the time. He often had to make do with shots from moving trains, some from the driving compartment of a DMU although none is included in this volume.

Such pictures were inevitably less than perfect but, given an interesting location and reasonable light, Priestley was able to go into action and, when something truly remarkable occurred, be it a fortuitous shaft of light, the interaction of people and the train, or simply an array of grandiose shapes, he would contrive to produce pictorial perfection.

During the production of this book I have once again been fortunate to work with Ian Brown LRPS, whose ability to interpret Priestley's negatives is unparalleled. The following is Ian's account of the task: 'I have tried to produce a set of prints which reveal all the detail and subtlety of each scene as Henry Priestley saw it through his camera's viewfinder. I found the negatives varied considerably; some printed easily while others were most reluctant to give up their secrets without a struggle. Sky areas usually proved the most problematical and often required up to six times more exposure than the rest of the negative. While strong blacks and pure whites are essential in a monochrome print, it is the mid tones which need to be properly balanced out if the photograph is to have any impact and reveal to the full all the details contained in the negative. Occasionally, a print had to be built up in stages, using masking techniques – the challenge being to ensure that it is not obvious to the viewer exactly how this was done. Prints created in this way were time-consuming to do, but the end, invariably, justified the means.'

Ian's prints are so good that Henry, in most cases, had never seen his pictures portrayed so well. Another delightful aspect of this book's production was the pleasant surprise he got as the various batches of prints were taken to him. He had little detailed knowledge of which negatives Milepost had acquired and the sudden appearance of a superb print of a picture he had taken upwards of fifty years ago evoked a flood of memories and associations. It was wonderful to see Henry's face light up as he was handed the prints; 'I remember that day,' he would say enthusiastically before continuing to provide chapter and verse on all the related issues. Fortunately the tape recorder was quietly whirring away alongside.

A Priestley picture is rarely about the locomotive; this is usually but a player on the stage. And yet, in spite of this, Priestley often manages to capture their full majesty, whether exerting great power and animation or suggesting a quiet dignity. Priestley seems to have eschewed the most popular types, and studies of LNER A4s, LMS 'Duchesses', and Great Western 'Kings', along with locations like Crewe, Clapham Junction and London Bridge, or any of the capital's great terminals, are rare among his work. It could be argued that the paucity of these subjects constituted a weakness in his approach. However, Priestley made the logical decision that, since so many others were concentrating on the most overt trains and places, he would cover the greater part of the railway which, by comparison, was being ignored.

Priestley the stylist was never better portrayed than by the prolific use of his two sons, whose appearance in pictures engenders all the magic of Cuneo's mouse. Clutching their train-spotting *abc*s, they are seen in a huge variety of interesting guises which must have been stage-managed, despite Henry's casual claim that they were placed within the picture area so he could 'keep his eye on them'. No other photographer in railway history attempted anything similar.

Priestley's pictures are like musical scores or literary manuscripts: they need to be read and are best reflected upon individually. They require concentration. In volume form like this, they may tend to look repetitive but the value of each individual picture lies in the story that it tells, as from each scene there flows a wealth of anecdote and historical associations. Priestley is a great story-teller.

I find a pictorial relationship between Henry Priestley and L.S. Lowry; both recorded a world according to their own personal perceptions. It was a world in a state of flux; a world which could not endure and one which would soon vanish without trace. Priestley's railwayscapes are now as extinct as Lowry's industrialscapes. Such pictures will become a focus for future generations to see the footprints of man's past which, as the aeons unfold, will become of intense relevance and interest to those who will be born in the technological wonderland which lies ahead. Perspectives are in a constant state of change and a Priestley picture and a Lowry painting will be of equal interest and value for their intense evocations of a legendary bygone age.

To know and work with Henry Priestley is a privilege. His sense of order, discipline, precision and enthusiasm, mixed with a wry sense of humour, form a constant inspiration and it is entirely fitting and fully characteristic that, despite his advanced years, he remains active in railway and tramway photography.

So great is his mental precision that he approaches everything with an air of caution, never forgetting that he may not have fully grasped the reality of a situation or remark. He does not jump to immediate conclusions, however great the temptation would be to lesser mortals. But once convinced that he is being confronted with inaccuracy, mischief or chicanery, he will deflate its puff in one carefully aimed sardonic sentence loaded with delightful irony.

Priestley's sense of order is reflected in the meticulous way in which he annotates every picture he takes. Place, date, locomotive number and depot allocation, the train it is working and direction in which the camera was facing, are all recorded, along with the exposure details. He even scratched with a pin the essential details on the margins of many negatives – complete with his signed initials! This is in marked contrast with most established railway photographers of the past who made few, if any, notes at all. The importance of these records cannot be overstated and it is particularly sad that, in the sell-off, a few of his precious notes have gone astray. This has led to a lack of information on some subjects and, in a few – fortunately rare – instances, a subject which cannot be identified at all.

Henry continues to live a peaceful and happy life with Margaret, his bride of over sixty years. He is immensely enthusiastic about the publication of this book and has contributed much to it by spending many long hours providing information and recalling, with remarkable clarity, facts and incidents from his seventy-five years as a photographer. My meetings and interviews with Henry have always concluded with a delightful trip to a nearby café for tea and muffins, and these occasions, along with the appreciation of his art, have greatly enriched my life.

Finally, Henry Priestley – quite rightly and with due respect – has exercised full editorial control of everything written in this book. But there is one final sentence in which I would like to reserve the author's prerogative to remain as written: 'That Henry Priestley is an "Olympian" cannot be disputed but, in plain English, he is also a genius.'

Colin Garratt,
Milepost 92½,
Newton Harcourt,
Leicestershire,
May 2000

An Appeal from Milepost 92½

Henry Priestley's legacy of railway negatives was sold piecemeal during the mid-1990s, unlike his British tramway pictures which are held exclusively by the National Tramway Museum at Crich. It is Milepost's remit to put together a representative selection of Henry Priestley's railway work in one co-ordinated library. This endeavour has Henry Priestley's support and co-operation. Widespread assistance from individuals nationwide has already allowed considerable progress to be made, which in turn has enabled books like this to be produced.

We appeal to anyone who has Priestley negatives in their collection, or knows where any are located, to contact Milepost with a view to some of them being transferred to the Priestley archive whether in the form of donations, purchases or exchange for other negatives. The totality of Henry Priestley's railway work constitutes a national heirloom and Milepost consider it vital to conserve, in digital form, a properly co-ordinated representative selection of his work in one permanent collection to be maintained, under his name, for posterity. Contact: Colin Garratt, Milepost 92½, Newton Harcourt, Leicestershire, England, LE8 9FH, tel: +44 (0)116 259 2068.

1. Associated Scenes

So monumental was Priestley's task that he was unable to visit many places more than once. Had he been a full-time photographer the situation would doubtless have been different as enormous changes were wrought during his most active years. Combining his responsibilities as a headmaster with the needs of a family, it is little short of miraculous that he achieved so much. This is especially true when one considers that railways were not his only photographic interest. He studied and photographed ancient and medieval architecture as well as railed transport which included trams. It is fitting that almost his entire tramway legacy, which covered nearly every system in Britain, is now under the custodianship of the National Tramway Museum in Crich, and experts such as Glyn Wilton and Ian Yearsley will readily attest to my belief that Priestley's pictures constitute the finest visual record ever made of Britain's tramways.

Fortunately, Priestley's chosen profession provided extended holidays and herein fate provided an opportunity exactly as it had done for the Revd A.W.C. Mace, whose photographic legacy is also vested with Milepost. Priestley's inspiration from the writings of T.R. Perkins in *The Railway Magazine* included an awareness of the inherent difficulties of how this Henley-in-Arden chemist, with only one half-day a week and Sundays at his disposal, could possibly have achieved his ambition of travelling over every railway line in Britain.

This chapter is distinctive in revealing that, on occasions, Henry was able to incorporate into his *oeuvre* repeated scenes, some taken as much as thirty years apart.

Opposite, above: The first of two classic pictures Henry made on a journey from Nottingham to London Marylebone over the GC main line. This was a time when the traditional LNER A3s, V2s and B1s had given way to more cosmopolitan motive power and his train was double headed by two closely related 4–6–0s; a former LMS 'Black 5' and a BR Standard 5. This is understandably one of Henry's favourite pictures; it is a dramatic evocation of one of the many motive power phases the GC went through during its short life. Notice the powerful composition in which the two locomotives are echoed by the station nameboard and lamps.

Opposite, below: Within the hour Priestley had made a second masterpiece on that afternoon as, upon arrival at Marylebone, he caught the two 4–6–0s simmering quietly in the terminal station. This was one of the negatives which Ian Brown had enormous problems with and nearly gave up, but his inimitable perseverance produced this splendid result.

On 9.6.65 BR 'Britannia' 4–6–2 No. 70021 *Western Star* stands at Oxenholme with an Up passenger. At this time the West Coast main line was electrified only as far north as Weaver Junction. Oxenholme Number 2 box served the station and the junction of the Windermere branch – Number 1 box lay further up the main line. LNW boxes were numbered from Number 1, the nearest to Euston.

On the same day, ex-LMS Stanier 2–6–4T No. 42613, bearing a Wigan Springs Branch shed-plate, waits to depart from Oxenholme with the 12.15 to Windermere.

A lovely view of Yatton, looking north, on 31 March 1926, and the second oldest picture in this volume. The stopping train in the platform is headed by former Great Western 'Bulldog' No. 3451 *Pelican*. Passengers are changing for trains to Wells and Clevedon.

Over thirty years later, little had changed at Yatton. The platform for Clevedon, with its 1400 class, 0–4–2T is on the left while the Wells platform, on the right, has a 4500 class, 2–6–2T receiving attention from the traditional GWR water tank. One suspects that the camera has caught Henry's two boys in the act of 'cabbing' the 4500.

Henry Priestley wrote an extended caption to cover these two pictures which I set out verbatim:

The first shows the north end of the Great Northern station with Retford North signal-box and GC gantry, with approach signals on the left. The sharp curve with check rails in the foreground enabled the GC trains (formerly MS&L) to use Retford station en route from Manchester to Grimsby and Cleethorpes; also GN expresses to link King's Cross and Sheffield. To the right (out of the picture) was the notorious GCR/GNR flat crossing; the local line had precedence over the GN main line, pre-dating it by several years. I frequently used Retford flat crossing in the east/west direction between 1932 and 1944 in the 'Mid-Day Fish' (three carriages and several vans) from Grimsby to Leicester GC, which avoided both Retford and Sheffield. In more recent years the flat crossing and the curve in the picture, (Whisker Hill), have been replaced by an underpass.

The picture opposite shows Ordsall crossing Retford; immediately behind the camera was the GN/GC flat crossing.

Parkstone is located at milepost 112, between Bournemouth and Poole on the former LSW main line from Waterloo to Weymouth. On 20 August 1962 'King Arthur' class 4–6–0 No. 30782 *Sir Brian* is seen approaching with a Down goods as an industrial saddle tank scuttles across the interchange sidings.

This companion to the previous picture concentrates on the 'King Arthur' and the station nameboard, the elusive saddle tank having, by this time, disappeared. Henry recalled, unsupported by notes, that the industrial line dipped under the main line to serve a quarry, whose stone was brought to the exchange siding alongside the station.

2.   Priestley at Large

The following pages encompass Priestley's mainstream work. Most of his pictures depicted steam-hauled trains simply because they were the norm at the time, and not as an end in themselves. Priestley was fully aware that to most photographers of the railway scene steam locomotives were a deity within themselves and capturing their glory was their prime motive. And, as Henry informed me on several occasions, they did it superbly; one only has to look at the masterpieces of men like Eric Treacy, Maurice Earley, E.R. Weathersett or H.C. Casserley. Priestley was not interested in repeating what others had done so successfully, but rather concentrated on what they had missed, i.e. the railway at large and, as Chapter 5 shows, some of the best Priestleys do not contain a train at all.

Priestley took a similar view with his trams; realising that other workers like W.A. Camwell and Maurice O'Connor concentrated primarily on tram portraits, Priestley put his trams into context, carefully including the ornate overheads and trackwork, the busy streets through which they passed in all their teeming architectural and commercial diversity and, not least, the people. Into this glorious potpourri came the tram, sympathetically depicted but invariably as a player on a stage rather than the virtuoso in its own right. He treated his railway scenes in exactly the same way. Henry's meticulous discipline and structured approach to life enabled him to move freely on his travels and embrace railways, tramways and architecture, all at the same time and with the dexterity of a juggler on stage or an old time 'one-man band'. He brought each scene to life, distilling its essential characteristics, and often all in a few grabbed moments of opportunity. He was well aware of running a race against time and, in the later years, when railway closures were becoming commonplace, he often had to seize or make an opportunity to visit some threatened section of line, sometimes arriving within a few days of closure.

There were exceptions, such as the one or two weeks' sojourn in Duns when, combined with a family holiday, he was able to cover many diverse locations ranging from remote branch lines to the East Coast main line and the Waverley route; the rare picture of the 'Pullman Express' at Fallodon and the scene at Hawick shed are good examples of many successful pictures made on that trip.

Writing as a professional photographer myself, it is abundantly clear how much energy Priestley needed to be 'at large' for so long and over so diverse an area – not to mention his foreign adventures. It is the same energy which enables him to continue working today; now in his nineties, he remains active as Britain's oldest railway photographer. As recently as April 2000, when we were preparing the text for this book, he declared over tea and muffins that this coming summer he was planning trips to the west coast of Scotland, making his base at the former Railway Hotel at Glasgow Central. Also, a trip was planned to cover the new Croydon tram system once that had come into full operation.

This is clearly the stuff of legend, and I commend the pictures within this chapter to you, not as an archive from a photographer of yesteryear but as part of an ongoing creativity and inspiration.

Opposite: This is one of Priestley's comparatively rare portrait format scenes and was taken at Burwell on the former Great Eastern Railway. The engine is ex-GE 2–4–0 No. 62796, a Cambridge engine, ready to leave for Mildenhall on 2.8.56. The E4s were a late flowering of this early passenger wheel arrangement and were the last examples of this type to remain in British service.

Many locomotive types, mainly in a run-down condition, were tried on Sheffield–Nottingham–Marylebone expresses in the post-war years. Two successful types were Gresley's V2, as pictured here heading an Up passenger train, and Stanier's 'Black 5s'. The GC line was built to approximately the Berne loading gauge, intended ultimately to connect Manchester and London with Paris via a Channel tunnel – in 1900! Rothley was one of the GCR's standard island platform stations and mostly well tended as here. It is still well kept today as part of the preserved GCR.

Crewkerne station, on the LSWR main line from Waterloo to the west of England, sporting a square-section signal-box with small windows and a truly magnificent station building. This study, taken on 6 September 1959, shows 'Battle of Britain' Pacific No. 34109 *Sir Trafford Leigh-Mallory* with the 3.20 Exeter to Yeovil Junction on a mixed train comprising passenger vehicles and milk tanks. Milk traffic from the West Country was an important commodity on this route, as it was on other main lines, especially the Great Western from Whitland which, at one time, was served by several dedicated milk trains nightly.

Repton and Willington station was located on the former Midland Railway, 6 miles south of Derby on the main line to Bristol. It had Spartan accommodation by MR standards and, when Henry first knew it, the V-shaped station nameboard showed 'Willington', followed by 'Alight for Repton School'. An MR 3F 0–6–0, with an approaching goods, completes the scene.

Rose Grove on the former L&Y system had a busy mineral yard and loco shed which was one of the last in Britain to retain steam traction. The station is still in use but, inevitably, much reduced. In this scene, on 28 August 1959, ex-WD 'Austerity' No. 90633 heads a mineral working with former LMS 4F, 0–6–0 No. 44460 in the background, left.

Ollerton, on the Nottinghamshire Coalfield, was formerly on the LDECR and later Great Central. Almost every station in the area had its own colliery with approach line and controlling signal-box. In this scene, looking west, a former War Department 'Austerity' 2–8–0 is seen at Ollerton Colliery signal-box, working light engine and van on 5 June 1965.

Opposite, above: The LBSCR's Hayling Island branch included Langston Bridge which imposed a severe restriction on what kind of engine could operate over it. The diminutive Brighton 'Terriers' were the favoured power until the end of steam and here one of these celebrated tanks pulls into Langston station. The gardens alongside are reminiscent, and possibly part, of the 'Dig for Victory' campaign in the Second World War. Notice the line of now vintage road vehicles waiting for the 'Terrier' to pass over the level crossing.

Opposite, below: The two centre tracks in this north-looking view of Bargoed station were originally the Rhymney Railway's main line from Cardiff to Rhymney. In this view of 18.4.62, GW 0–6–0PT No. 3706 is seen taking water on the left, at the head of a Newport to Brecon through train. GW 0–6–2T No. 5601 is seen, right, with a sister engine standing centre. The engines face in the uphill direction, as did all the valley's locomotives, in order to ensure a proper cover of water over the firebox when climbing the many steep gradients.

The LB&SCR station at Polegate looking east with Billinton Class E4 0–6–2T No. 32566, allocated to 75A, Brighton, at the head of the 4.59 Eastbourne to Hailsham train on 13 June 1957. Besides being the junction for Eastbourne, Polegate was also the junction for a line (now dismantled) to London via Eridge on the first leg of which this train was about to embark.

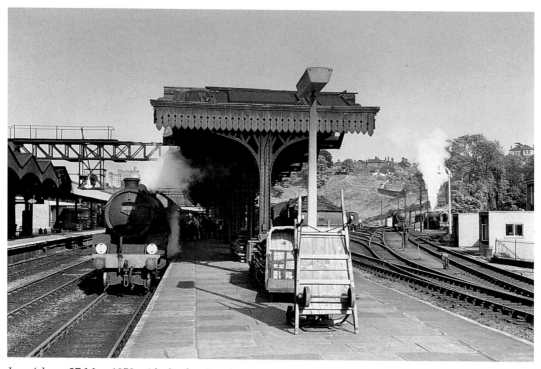

Ipswich on 27 May 1958 with the first B1 class 4–6–0 No. 61000 *Springbok* in the main platform, with B12s, Nos 61561 and 61554, and B17, No. 61622 *Alnwick Castle* on shed visible to the right. Ipswich is a main city and junction on the former Great Eastern main line where it forks for Norwich and Yarmouth. H.B.P. points out that the recently increased traffic to and from Felixstowe has taxed the facilities here.

A scene of the former NER's station at Malton, looking north-east and showing the Down line, with two platform faces, under the overall roof and the Up platform line outside. The engine is Darlington-based V2 No. 60808, with the 6.30 Scarborough to Doncaster train on 11 August 1962.

This bold camera viewpoint gives a magnificent view of Abercynon TVR station in its highly characteristic Welsh valleys setting. In this scene, taken on 12 June 1962, GW 0–6–2T No. 6642 heads south with a coal train. Abercynon shed, AYN, is hidden on the left.

To me, this is one of the most charming and evocative pictures in this volume; sentiments with which Henry agrees. The scene is Chipping Norton station with GW 2–4–0T No. 457 on 4 August 1934. When discussing this picture, Henry commented: 'The train is a two-coach shuttle service from Kingham on the Cotswold line. Kingham was originally Chipping Norton Junction, until the line was extended at both ends to join Cheltenham and Banbury. It was then used by the "Ports to Ports Express" from Barry to Newcastle upon Tyne via the BR, GWR, GC and NER. A Kingham avoiding line enabled it to bypass that station while still serving Chipping Norton which, thereby, twice daily, saw GW Moguls from Canton and from Gloucester.'

Glasgow Polmadie-based Drummond 0–6–0 No. 57369 stands at Eglinton Street station with a passenger train on 10 August 1957. Eglinton Street (at milepost 1) was the first station out of Glasgow Central and was on both 'inner' and 'outer' routes. The Cathcart Circle was, in fact, pear-shaped with Glasgow at the stem (the north end). The points for the Cathcart Circle lay at the south end of Eglinton Street station.

The former L&Y station at Shaw & Crompton, looking north on 29.8.57. A passenger special from Blackpool to Oldham and Rochdale is headed by 'Black 5' 4–6–0 No. 45156 *Ayrshire Yeomanry*, one of only four 'Black 5s' to be named. The typical Lancashire cotton mill in the background was still there on H.B.P.'s visit in 1998.

This scene of the LNWR's Manchester Exchange station shows a BR-built Standard 5 4–6–0 backing to Patricroft loco shed after bringing in a train from North Wales. Exchange's bay platforms are in view; what was the longest platform in Britain is further back, leading to Victoria's platform 11.

The ex-Caledonian Railway's Glasgow Central High Level station, looking north on 6 April 1959. 'Princess Coronation' Pacific No. 46232 *Duchess of Montrose* stands at platform 1, the main departure platform, with the south bound 'Royal Scot', as sister engine No. 46246 'City of Manchester' waits in the background with the 10.25 to Birmingham. The scene is completed by BR Standard 2–6–4Ts No. 80058, facing the camera, and No. 80129, bunker first, in the end platform, left. Notice the customary group of train-spotters at the south end of platform 1.

This scene is another of Henry's great favourites and shows a very different element in his photography. The subject is ex-LMS Buxton-based 4F, No. 44339 at the head of a Buxton to Derby local goods in the Peak District. The train is caught on Monsal Dale Viaduct and is about to enter the tunnel; a scene dated 14.9.57. This picture is also exceptional in being one of Priestley's few viaduct scenes, albeit from a somewhat unconventional angle.

The Great Western's terminal station at Minehead on 1 September 1959, with 5101 class 2–6–2T No. 4128 at the head of the 12.20 to Taunton. Busily shunting the adjacent goods yard is 2251 class 0–6–0 No. 2250, having worked in on a pick-up goods. Henry Priestley points out that this was another key station closed under Beeching wherein the same comments apply as those made about Swanage (see p. 41). Fittingly, Minehead also forms part of a preserved system and remains in busy use, albeit shamefully, there is no regular connecting service running through to Taunton.

The single-platform terminus of the shuttle service from Killin Junction on the Callander and Oban line. The engine has gravity-shunted its single bogie composite as the run-round loop is outside the station. Presumably, the authorities were aware of, and permitted, this practice provided no passengers were on board. The engine is ex-CR 0–4–4T No. 55195, with the 1.42 to Killin Junction on 3.4.59.

A scene packed full of atmosphere and interest showing Thurston, looking east on 28.5.58. J39 class 0–6–0 No. 64800, with a pick-up goods, is to the left while B12, 4–6–0 No. 61573 approaches with the 2.24 Ipswich to Cambridge train. The entrance to this station is at road level, below the line. Thurston lies 22¾ miles from Ipswich and 7 miles from Bury St Edmunds.

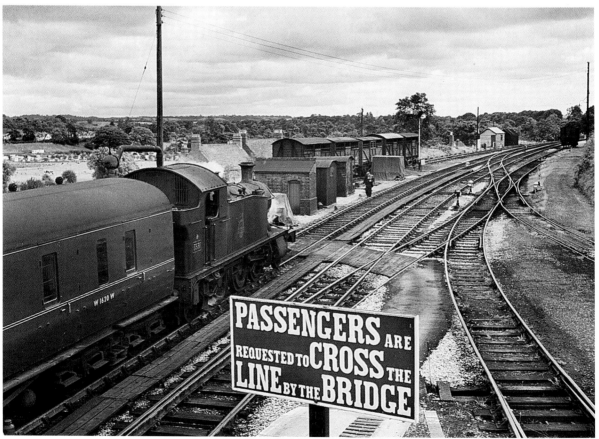

The former LSWR station at Creekmoor showing evidence of the Southern Railway's reinforced concrete refurbishment programme. The engine is an ex-LSWR M7 class 0–4–4T, with the 2.30 Bournemouth to Brockenhurst train on 12 August 1962.

Opposite, above: The Caledonian Railway's Beattock station was once the starting point for the long, formidable climb to Beattock Summit and the adjacent loco shed turned out banking engines for many of the trains. It was also the junction for the 2-mile long Moffat branch and, in this scene of 14 April 1954, Pickersgill 0–4–4T No. 55237 waits with the Moffat train. The three signals are, left to right, main line, cross over and Moffat branch. Today, the rigours of the long climb, the loco shed, the Moffat branch, the semaphore signals and, of course, the station itself, have all gone. H.B.P. points out that Scotrail might well create a Parkway station where Beattock once stood to serve the now-important area of Moffat and provide an intermediate station on the long section from Lockerbie to Carstairs – a distance of some 50 miles of main line electrified railway with no station.

Opposite, below: A pre-preservation scene on the Severn Valley line with GW Class 4575 Prairie tank, No. 5538, at Bridgnorth, with a train from Shrewsbury to Kidderminster, on 22 August 1961.

Gresley's LNER V2 class of 2–6–2s were known as the 'engines which won the war' with their superb hauling capabilities and ready turns of speed. They were one of the most successful mixed traffic locomotives of all time and here No. 60957, an Edinburgh St Margaret's engine, is seen at the head of a heavy coal train. Henry's notes on this picture have gone astray and, most unusually, he is unable to cite the exact location but says, 'I took such a shot at Longniddry, could it be this?' It is certainly believed to be on the East Coast main line south of Edinburgh.

The M&GN Joint Railway's Gayton Road station was on the main line some 5½ miles east of King's Lynn; for much of the day it was a request stop and in this picture, dated 28.7.56, Ivatt 2–6–0 No. 43108 – a 31D South Lynn engine – is seen with the 10.05 Yarmouth Beach to Peterborough train. H.B.P. mentions that the GNR was responsible for the signalling; the high centre balance somersault signal arm, with eye-level repeater, became standard on the GNR after the Abbot's Ripton accident some 130 years ago. There, an accumulation of snow on the standard signal arm caused it to fall into a 60° position and give a false 'clear' reading.

Garstang and Catterall on the former LNWR section of the West Coast main line. A few semi-fasts stopped to connect with Fylde trains to Knott End for Fleetwood, using the slow line on the left. A 'Black 5', No. 45343 (8D), sports a fine head of smoke as it hastens an Up fitted freight on 6.4.57.

Tondû, GWR, with typical mineral trains headed by pannier tanks Nos 8710, on a train in the foreground, and 3616, to the rear. Dated 12.6.62, this picture was made during one of Henry's extended trips to the Welsh valleys. Tondû was an important concentration yard, complete with station, some t3 miles from Bridgend. It had the locomotive shed for Bridgend and served three valleys, along with the through line to Porthcawl. On the left is a typical rear view of a GWR fixed-distant semaphore, with no spectacle glass.

The former LB&SCR station at Lewes looking east and featuring Billinton Class K Mogul No. 32343, a Brighton engine, with a permanent way train. Leaving on the right is an EMU forming the 12.45 Victoria to Eastbourne in a scene dated 13.6.57. Henry apologises for the confusion of signals; the two gantries, so unceremoniously pushed together in this view, are uncharacteristic, but it was unavoidable.

Gloucester Midland station looking south-west along the handsome contours of former LMS 'Jubilee' No. 45627 *Sierra Leone*, a Derby engine, with the 7.35 Nottingham to Bristol on 26.9.59. Note the rare Midland signal-box on the gantry and the main road level crossing beyond. The latter was instrumental in ultimately having this station closed; all Birmingham to Britsol trains using the ex-MR route today either reverse at Gloucester (ex-GW) or use the GW avoiding line from the engine shed on to Tuffley Junction, so avoiding reversal.

Henry Priestley was not accustomed to photographing London terminals but this scene of 'Schools' class 4–4–0 No. 30902 *Wellington*, at the head of the 12.54 Waterloo to Basingstoke on 30.12.59, was specially taken to show this class in action, from Basingstoke shed.

Ex-LNER Pacific No. 60159 *Bonnie Dundee*, an Edinburgh Haymarket engine, leads the Up 'Queen of Scots' at Newcastle Central on 29 December 1954. On this day, H.B.P. photographed V2 No. 60835 *The Green Howard* etc. at this station and also went to Prudhoe. He recalls the day with great clarity almost fifty years later.

It was unusual for Henry Priestley to take such unashamed locomotive portraits but his interest here clearly lay in the veteran Aspinall, ex-L&Y 0–6–0 No. 52509, seen here at its home shed of Workington on 5.9.54, in company with 'Black 5' No. 45092 displaying an 11A, Carnforth, shed-plate. This depot supplied 'Black 5s' to work to Lancashire stations via Preston and 0–6–0s for FR mineral workings; also NER mineral workings via Belah Viaduct to County Durham.

The Caledonian Railway's Gleneagles station was the alighting point for the luxurious Railway Hotel. It was a location which attracted tourists from around the world and the platforms were decorated accordingly, and were provided with luggage lifts. Here, ex-LNER V2 No. 60958 is seen with the 3.30 Aberdeen to Edinburgh train, with the Crieff railbus waiting on the left, on 31.8.61. This was one of the many railway hotels sold during the Prime Minister Macmillan years, along with many railway ferry services, under a programme known as 'hiving off'.

Kirkby-in-Ashfield Central station looking north, with an excursion train in the Up platform headed by K3 class 2–6–0 No. 61982 (40E), with the 1.28, Saturdays only, excursion returning from Cleethorpes. The line, some 11 miles long, connected Kirkby South junction with Edwinstowe, opening up a rich coalfield district.

The former Great Eastern station at Finningham, looking north on 28.5.58 with J17 class 0–6–0 No. 65542 on a pick up goods. Finningham is on the GER main line, 86 miles from Liverpool Street and 20 miles from Norwich Thorpe.

A Collett 2251 class 0–6–0 stands in Pensford, Great Western station with the 10.20 Bristol to Frome train via Radstock on 22.8.57. The engine is No. 2213, allocated to 82B – Bristol, St Philip's Marsh. These engines were the successors to the famous Dean Goods 0–6–0s which, in actuality, were mixed traffic engines. Pensford was approximately 7 miles from Bristol and 18 miles from Frome.

The L&Y station at Todmorden looking east on 29.8.57, with ex-LMS 'Black 5' No. 44928 (27A) on the 5.10 Leeds Central to Liverpool Exchange and former L&Y 2–4–2T No. 50777 (56E) with the 6.10 to Halifax. Henry pointed out that the station nameboard advises passengers how to stay in that county – Burnley, Accrington and Blackburn are all in Lancashire. Passengers who continued direct came to Hebden Bridge, which is in Yorkshire.

Frome station has the only surviving country example of a Brunel-type overall roof. Former Great Western 2251 class 0–6–0 No. 2213 is seen at the head of the 3.17 train to Yatton via Wells on 21 August 1957.

A truly delightful study of the former LSWR station at Swanage. In the summer season this was a busy seaside terminus until Beeching's accountants found that Swanage's takings did not cover expenses. The fact that travellers booked return tickets to Swanage from all over the system, which were not reflected in the station's takings, was of no avail in preventing closure. M7 class 0–4–4Ts worked the line for many years and here, on 4 September 1959, we see No. 30104, with sister engine No. 30106. The station is now the headquarters of a successful preserved railway and an M7 has, once again, returned to its metals.

This splendid evocation highlights the GWR style nameboard at Norton Fitzwarren, in a view dated 19.5.56. An express approaches on the Up main, with the engine bearing the train number for the information of signal staff and control. Henry comments: 'In the early 1930s, the Chancellor of the Exchequer (Right Hon. Winston Churchill) remitted duty on first class fares provided the railways spent the capital equivalent on improvements. The GWR quadrupled the line from Norton Fitzwarren to Cogload Junction and made the latter non-conflicting.' Thereafter, passengers changed at Taunton rather than here.

Murrow was located on the GER/GN joint line from Lincoln to March. In this scene, looking north, it is crossed by the M&GN route and the down goods, running east to South Lynn, is headed by Ivatt 2–6–0 No. 43081, a Neasden engine. The date is 28.2.59. In their heyday, these engines successfully worked all the M&GN line traffic from Leicester and Peterborough in the west to Norwich and Yarmouth in the east. Note the BR ARP type signal-box with its thick reinforced concrete roof. These reinforcements were built in the war years to render the boxes less susceptible to aerial damage.

Opposite, above: A view of Beeston station, looking north-east towards Nottingham. As recently as 1993, the station building on the Down side bore the date 1847 and is, presumably, the subject of a preservation order. One is tempted to say that the wooden sleepers on the platform have some connection with the creosoting depot which, at the time of this picture, had a small fleet of diesel locomotives for internal use.

Opposite, below: Shepton Mallet on the S&DJR looking south with a train of limestone in open wagons. The signal-box of LSWR appearance is consistent as the S&DJR was signalled by the LSWR.

The Caledonian Railway's Mount Florida station on Glasgow's Cathcart Circle with BR Standard 2–6–4T No. 80114, a Polmadie engine, at the head of a passenger train on 6.8.55. This was a well-designed island platform station in a densely built-up area making the most of limited space. H.B.P. points out that the Cathcart Circle was an early example of a purely commuter service. Mount Florida, at under 3 miles from Glasgow Central, was the fifth station on the 'outer rail' from Glasgow Central (exclusive) and, at under 6 miles, was the eighth stop on the 'inner rail'. The circle stations were also served by non circle trains, from outer suburban places.

Seaton Junction was located 145 miles from Waterloo on the L&SWR main line. The station, which is now demolished completely, was the starting point for the 4¾-mile branch to Seaton, which still flourishes at its outer end as the 'Seaton Tramway', a narrow gauge line worked by miniature electric trams. This scene shows Seaton Junction on 2 September 1959 with M7 0–4–4T No. 30045 shunting the Seaton branch train. One wonders if the solitary boy standing on the platform is one of Henry's. This is unproven but probably not, as his stance is too quiescent.

The L&SWR station at Broadstone had generous provision for the S&DJR trains on the left and for its own locals (Salisbury to Bournemouth) on the right. The vigorously active M7 is fitted with a Westinghouse pump and dome-mounted safety valves. She is No. 30056, a Bournemouth engine, caught on 20 August 1962 with the 12.08 Brockenhurst to Bournemouth train using the old route, via Ringwood, later superseded by the line via Sway.

Shifnal looking west as former Great Western, 'Hall' class 4–6–0 No. 6922 *Burton Hall* approaches with a passenger train. This station is situated well above road level, with the offices down below. Shifnal is located between Wolverhampton and Shrewsbury but is now part of Telford New Town.

Newhaven shed on 12 July 1947. In pride of position is No. 2037 *Selsey Bill*, one of the classic Marsh LBSCR, H1 class 4–4–2 Atlantics. This shed had several LBSCR Atlantics allocated for working the boat trains from London Victoria to connect with the Newhaven to Dieppe sailings. A later sister engine stands in the centre in the form of H2 class No. 2423, *The Needles*. The resemblance between these engines and those of Ivatt on the GNR is striking. On the left is former LBSCR Billinton E4 class 0–6–2 No. 2508.

Coalburn station was once the terminus of one of the Caledonian's more remote Lanarkshire branches, running some 16 miles south from Hamilton Central. In this scene on 4 April 1959, we see Fairburn 2–6–4T No. 42129, a 66B, Hamilton engine, with the 12.50 from Glasgow Central. Note the unique Caledonian route indicator on the bufferbeam. H.B.P. points out that the origin of the station name comes from burn – a river – in this coal-producing area.

Opposite, above: Eyemouth station was the terminus of the 3-mile NBR branch from Burnmouth, which was itself on the East Coast main line 5½ miles north of Berwick-on-Tweed. Burn and Eye are both rivers and Eyemouth a fishing village which lies at sea level below the East Coast main line. In this scene the branch was being worked by one of Gresley's ever-popular J39 class mixed traffic 0–6–0s, No. 64925.

Opposite, below: The NER's station at Thorner was 8¾ miles from Leeds (New – as opposed to Wellington and Central). The Thorner line, via Wetherby, afforded a through route from London to Harrogate without reversal at Leeds Central. Of particular interest here is the typical NER all-brick signal-box. The train is headed by one of Gresley's J39 class mixed traffic 0–6–0s of which 289 examples were built between 1926 and 1941.

The MR's station at Rotherham featuring a local train to Sheffield. 'T'owd road' to Chesterfield, via the Rother Valley, is in the foreground. The engine is Stanier 2–6–2T No. 40140 – a Royston engine – with the 8.41 from Leeds on 18.6.55. Today, Leeds to Sheffield local trains are diverted via Castleford (reverse), Wakefield Kirkgate and Barnsley covering a longer mileage.

This nostalgic scene of Preston (North End) on 10 April 1955 shows 'Black 5' No. 45387 – a Willesden engine – along with 'Jubilee' class No. 45634 *Trinidad* from Crewe North. The immaculate 'Jubilee' reveals loving care on behalf of her home depot rather than being ex-works and is typical of the elbow grease expended on these locomotives during much of their working lives. The unusual signal gantry consists of four starters and four distants; all four dolls with LNWR finials and all eight arms of similar size in LNW type corrugated steel.

Six Mile Bottom is 7¾ miles from Cambridge and 6 miles from Newmarket (perhaps contributing to its name). It saw through trains between Cambridge and Ipswich via Bury St Edmunds. In this picture, taken on 3 June 1952, K3 No. 61942 is seen with an Ipswich to Cambridge train. A delightful line of period road traffic waits at the crossing; the superb goods shed sports the traditional 'No Engine to Enter' sign while the revision of fares and holiday runabouts for 20 shillings are additionally evocative in this scene of half a century past.

The Midland Railway's Swinton station, 10 miles north of Sheffield, was the southern terminus of the Swinton and Knottingly joint line. In this view, looking south, ex-LMS 'Jubilee' No. 45699 *Galatea* – a Bristol engine – heads the Down 'Devonian' (8.45 ex-Plymouth) on 18 June 1955. The signals are clear for the Midland main line and 'on' for the GC curve to Mexborough. Note the characteristic reluctance of the lower semaphore to lift to its proper position.

The up 'Queen of Scots' Pullman approaches Fallodon siding behind A2 Pacific, No. 60516 *Hycilla* on 7 June 1960. Henry's camera on this occasion was an Agfa Sillette and the picture is one made during his sojourn at Duns. Henry suggests that the little-known Fallodon siding, near Christon Bank, was a road-side siding of earlier years due to the sparsity of stations on this NER section of the East Coast main line.

Woodford Halse (formerly Woodford and Hinton) was a typical Great Central 'London Extension' island platform plus (unusually) a single platform on the west for trains to Banbury and the S&MJ line. The stopping passenger train seen in the platform in this study, taken on 10 June 1957, is headed by L1 class No. 67789, a 38E (Woodford Halse) engine.

Possil station was located in the suburban and industrial area north of Glasgow and here we see Stanier 2–6–2T, No. 40176 at the head of a lunch-time special on 30.7.55. Possil had two stations originally, one Caledonian and one North British, and one was once known as Possilpark. Unfortunately this is another instance when H.B.P.'s notes have become separated from the negative and we are not certain which of the two stations this is. Henry found that neither of them was mentioned in his Bradshaw.

The former LSWR station at Honiton was located at the top of the formidable Honiton Bank. This view, looking east, features a post-war ARP type signal-box, along with 'West Country' Pacific No. 34033 *Chard*, heading the 12.46 Salisbury to Exeter local on 1 September 1958.

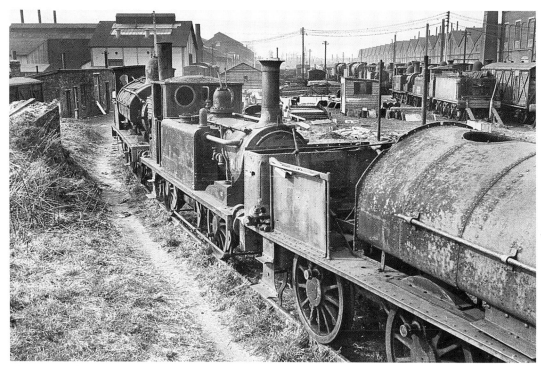

This wonderful composition of Eastleigh Works scrapyard was taken on 12 April 1947. In the foreground a Brighton 'Terrier', No. B683, is sandwiched between two LSWR saddle tanks, Nos 3332 and 3334. To the rear right stands Nos 2232 and 2233, a Stroudley Class D1. Introduced in 1873, scrapping of this type began in 1903. In the far distance a couple of ex-War Department 'Austerity' 2–8–0s can be seen.

February 28, 1959 was a sad day in railway history as it heralded the end of the M&GN Joint Railway system. Here, on the last day, Ivatt 2–6–0 No. 43161, allocated to 32F Yarmouth Beach, is seen approaching Weston with the 9.02 train from Yarmouth. Weston was located on one of the 'lines west', i.e. between Sutton Bridge and Bourne, 2 miles east of Spalding. Note the scribbled 'That's Yer Lot' headboard carried by the locomotive. The headboard had, apparently, been attached by local drivers as an epitaph.

3. Irish Recollections

This is one of Henry Priestley's 'Baroque' pictures. Rich in sumptuous detail, it is a photograph which, for me, releases an overwhelming surge of emotion. I would use the word 'made' rather than 'taken' on 6 August 1950 at Adelaide station which was the location for Belfast's locomotive depot. The GNR(I) T2 class 4–4–2T seen arriving is No. 139, with a local train from Lisburn.

Enniskillen, also on the GNR(I) network, was 116 miles from Dublin. This view of the running shed was taken on 11 August 1951, the main subject being SG3 class 0–6–0 No. 117, which is being prepared for taking a train to Londonderry. Seen in the right background is PP class No. 44, a handsome Victorian style 4–4–0. Notice on the far left the ancient coach in use as an enginemen's mess.

Opposite, above: Castleblayney on the GNR(I) network, 18 miles west of Dundalk on the former Irish North Western Line. The picture was taken from a Dundalk and Enniskillen to Londonderry train headed by U class 4–4–0 No. 198 which was crossing a Londonderry to Dundalk train hauled by U class 4–4–0 No. 202 *Louth*, built by Beyer Peacock in 1948. Castleblayney was the junction of an 18-mile rural line to Armagh. Henry often took pictures from trains, both stationary and moving, and this *genre* is perhaps the least successful of his entire output; understandably so as he was literally grabbing an opportunity. He mentions that when a train was stationary, as it was here, he would move along the corridor to adjust the salient features of the composition and so exercise greater control. The picture was taken on 11 April 1956.

Opposite, below: The former City of Dublin Junction Railway linked Amiens Street and Westland Row. On 13 August 1956 Henry took this view of Amiens Street cabin looking south-west with the GNR(I) terminus on the left. The engine is J15B No. 717, an Inchicore development of the J class 0–6–0s of the GSR.

One of the most endearing aspects of Priestley's work is the inclusion in so many of his pictures of his two small sons. The boys were growing up during the mid 1950s and '60s, a time when Henry was particularly active as both the steam age and the railway itself were being seen as increasingly obsolete. Many of Priestley's trips were done by car and his Wolseley can also be found in some of the pictures, occasionally with the door left open as if in a quick dash to obtain a picture, and then be off again to the next location.

Like Cuneo's mouse, the two boys add great distinction to his work; like the elusive mouse, their presence is not always obvious and they frequently have to be searched for. They are caught in a wide variety of poses, often clutching their *abc*s and avidly straining to read the number of an oncoming locomotive. Almost without exception the boys are placed with consummate skill like figures in a Lowry painting, except that in these pictures they often represent the only example of humanity for it is sadly noticeable how few people – passengers or staff – populate scenes which, only a decade earlier, would have been a thriving part of the community. Herein lay the excuse for Beeching's mischief under which the Tory government of the day absolved itself of its responsibility to provide properly co-ordinated transport for the nation in favour of unfettered road development. Accordingly, the Beeching Plan was evolved in which over 40 per cent of Britain's railway infrastructure was destroyed, so rendering the railway impotent in ever again playing a major role in handling the nation's freight. Priestley's pictures show the railway as it was before the vandalism began. Today, we are paying the price and seeking ineffectively to provide a system akin to what was destroyed. The same tenet applies to the national tramway network; and Priestley recalls vividly the *Daily Mail*'s long campaign to be rid of trams and, to a lesser extent, railways too.

It is an interesting reflection that the two boys seen in this chapter are now in their fifties and, not surprisingly, have retained their interest in, and knowledge of railways.

There is one other Lowry analogy I would like to make; exactly why were the boys included in the pictures? Henry's reply to this question has always been, 'so that I could keep an eye on them'. That is exactly the kind of reply Lowry would have made to such a question. But I suspect a far broader motive, for those boys add not just animation but, on many occasions, compositional balance. They are, in the absence of passengers, figures of the period and they behave in that way too, for they epitomise another essential element of the railway of that time, namely the national passion for train-spotting. This was a time when most boys were interested in either railways or football or, in many cases, both. The presence of Priestley's two sons in his pictures emphasises his skill as a photographer and as a communicator. As for 'having to keep an eye on them', this can be doubted; Priestley's boys would have been sufficiently disciplined to do as they were bidden. One only has to look at the errant urchins galloping across the shed yard in one of the plates to know, in the instant, that these were not Priestley's boys.

Opposite, above: This is perhaps my favourite scene of H.B.P.'s two boys, taken in 1951. Far from lurking in the shadows, they exert every bit as much pictorial importance as does the approaching LMS 4F 0–6–0. The location is Chesterfield Midland where the platform-mounted semaphore signal makes a superb contribution to the picture's rhythms. Notice the two water cranes dripping noisily behind the platform.

Opposite, below: Frisby station, MR, with Nottingham-based Stanier 8F No. 48064 at the head of a west-bound mineral train on 9.2.57. Here, H.B.P.'s two boys take an evocative stance, straining to see over the fence with notebooks at the ready.

H.B.P.'s boys have seldom been better placed than in this view, looking north at Ambergate on the former MR. They enthusiastically write down the number of passing Burton 'Crab' 2–6–0 No. 42825, one of several which were experimentally fitted with Lentz rotary cam poppet valves. Note that on this occasion they had a friend with them. Did Henry position the one gazing towards the camera in the bottom left-hand corner? If so, what about the one gazing from the picture's middle distance? Ambergate's celebrated triangular junction, with all six platforms in use, saw passenger trains from Derby to Chesterfield, Derby to Matlock and Matlock to Chesterfield. Today, this view would show the near platform only stripped of this attractive station building. Signal-boxes existed at all three points of the triangle. The north-western box can be seen distantly. A scene dated 15 September 1956.

The delightful station at Grange-over-Sands was on the Furness Railway's main line and in this view, taken on 25 June 1953, 'Black 5' No. 45046 is seen arriving with the 3.40 train from Carnforth to Barrow. This station was restored by BR some thirty years later.

Elmton and Cresswell looking north as a Worksop to Nottingham local arrives behind a former LT& SR 4–4–2T in 1951. These Tilbury Tanks worked this service until 1952, albeit unsatisfactorily, but this was true wherever they went after Derby had transferred them away from their original LTS line, which was flat and where they were fast, successful engines. They were underpowered and unsuitable for most other locations. Leicester Midland had one which was nicknamed 'Mrs Simpson'. It spent its years sitting in the roundhouse at Wigston; Toton had one and relegated it to shed pilot duties and Hellifield had four which they despatched to Durran Hill, the former Midland shed in Carlisle, where they stood rotting in the open air for many years. H.B.P. expresses surprise that Mansfield put up with them.

Clay Cross looking north. The near lines were part of the original North Midland Railway (Leeds to Derby). Far lines branch away to Nottingham via the Erewash Valley. Seen approaching is Stanier 8F No. 48395 – a 16C Kirkby engine with an Up minerals on 2.6.55.

A double-headed freight storms through Widmerpool on the Midland main line southwards from Nottingham to Melton with an ex-LMS 4F 0–6–0 piloting a former WD 'Austerity' 2–8–0. Is it a cop? The magic of train-spotting is evoked as one of Priestley's boys avidly checks his *abc*. The station house is typical of the stately designs on this alternative Midland Railway route from London to the North. The date is 5 November 1956 – fireworks night in more than one sense as this pair must have made a shattering audio-visual spectacle as witnessed by the onlookers in the background. Today, this section of line forms part of the Old Dalby test track and is to be electrified to test the new Virgin Pendolino high speed tilting trains.

Bustle, excitement and movement are revealed in this remarkable picture of Long Eaton station as it was prior to closure and Sawley Junction station being renamed Long Eaton. The departing train is headed by a former MR 'simple' 4–4–0 No. 40585, a Nottingham engine, at the head of a Chesterfield to Nottingham service on 21 February 1959. The Long Eaton Co-op van is a masterpiece in its own right. Notice the number of people using bikes and shanks's pony in those glorious years before mass motorisation.

Asfordby station on the MR line from Syston to Melton Mowbray with Kettering-based Stanier 8F No. 48069 at the head of a Down minerals on 9.2.57. On this same day, Henry visited Brooksby, Frisby and Widmerpool.

Clevedon was the terminus of the former GWR 3½-mile branch from Yatton and GW 4575 class 2–6–2T No. 5565, a Bristol, Bath Road 82A engine, is seen running round its train in readiness for the return journey to Yatton on 19.8.57.

Congresbury, less than 2 miles east of Yatton, GWR, was at the junction of two branch lines, to Blagdon (for the reservoir) and to Wells via Cheddar. Ivatt 2–6–0 No. 46506, allocated to 82B, Bristol, St Philip's Marsh, is seen shunting a pick-up goods on 19 August 1957.

Henry's two sons gaze admiringly as Ivatt 2–6–2T No. 41304 (71J) arrives at Pylle on the 5 o'clock Evercreech Junction to Highbridge train on 19 August 1957. Pylle, seen here looking east, was a former S&DJR station.

A view of the former Midland Railway station at Hunslet looking north towards Leeds as ex-LMS 4F No. 44467, allocated to 20B Stourton, propels a guards van to Stourton yard on 18.6.65.

This is another of H.B.P.'s favourite pictures and one whose atmosphere depends entirely on a grey, wet day. Henry emphasises that the cloud of smoke and steam would not be so visible had the weather been better. Taken on 16 June 1956, the scene depicts Gresley V2 class No. 60817 at Staveley Central station on the Great Central main line. One of Henry's boys takes up a gallant pose in the left foreground, eager to identify the emerging 2–6–2.

Ollerton was on the former Lancashire, Derbyshire & East Coast Railway, which was incorporated into the Great Central. This scene, taken on 4.12.54, depicts Robinson C13 class 4–4–2T No. 67437.

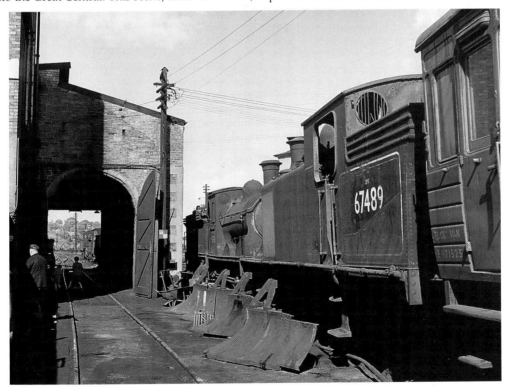

Henry's boys were to be found in some surprising positions but never better than in this Sunday scene at Hawick loco shed on the renowned Waverley Route from Carlisle to Edinburgh. Vindictively closed under Beeching despite enormous opposition, the Waverley Route was arguably one of the most beautiful lines in the world. Today, there is a strong feeling in many quarters that the route should be reopened. Here, on 9.6.60, former NB, C16 class 4–4–2T No. 67489 – allocated to Dundee, Tay Bridge – lies in store next to Hawick's own ex-NB, J36 class 0–6–0 No. 65316, which appears to be still in service. Note the line of snow ploughs in the foreground and the wooden-bodied engineers' coach on the right.

Wells (Somerset) was a former GW/S&DJR station and, in this view looking east, GW 2–6–2T No. 5525 is seen with the 9.35 train to Yatton, crossing a local pick-up goods with Ivatt 2–6–0 No. 46517 in charge on 21 August 1957.

Heckington, GNR, looking east, with a Boston to Grantham DMU No. 50044 on 29 May 1958. The somersault signals and the unique eight-sailed windmill add poetry to the scene.

5. Topography

The term 'railway photographer', as commonly used, is a generalisation. It is applied freely to those whose primary interest is locomotives – usually steam – or, at best, trains. Other elements obviously occur in such pictures but usually only to help emphasise the subject and not as entities in themselves. Priestley was a railway photographer in the true meaning of the term and, in the lovely evocations in this chapter, the infrastructure shows stronger without the distraction of a train. Interestingly though, the pictures retain the full vitality of the railway as a living entity and many conjure up that expectant atmosphere which precedes the arrival of a train.

It must be stated, however, that there are surprising omissions in Priestley's work; tunnels and viaducts are conspicuously absent, while detailed essays into the railway's rich architectural treasures are infrequent. This is particularly strange given Henry's vast photographic output on architecture. After the church, the railway is the largest owner of listed buildings of England. It is perhaps doubly strange that, given Priestley's race against time to record the fleeting aspects of the railway, he should have omitted architecture; many of the railway treasures – like the Doric Arch – have gone, while others have been disfigured, either by progress or neglect. Paradoxically, many of the churches Henry so lovingly recorded are much the same today and will long be so. At the very time of writing comes news of the heavy rebuilding of Rugby's magnificent London & North Western station, a breathtakingly beautiful example of the grandeur of its former owner. If only Priestley had concentrated on railway architecture instead of churches another valuable dimension would have been added to his name and legacy, not least since hardly any other photographers had covered this area. By comparison, church architecture has been adequately recorded.

Henry also tended to ignore the larger stations and junctions. The London termini do not feature in his work and he produced a better evocation of the essence of Henstridge, a remote S&DJR halt, than he ever did of Crewe! Perhaps he felt that other photographers had adequately covered the major centres whereas the secondary routes and branch lines were, by comparison, being overlooked. Nevertheless, the omission of such large and important railway centres stands in stark contrast to the thoroughness with which he pursued his ambitions on the network in general.

In reflecting on all that has occurred in Britain's two centuries of railway history we find a plethora of subjects which should have been better covered by the photographers of yesteryear, not least the people who, in all their rich diversity, ran the railway – father followed by son in successive generations of railway service.

To proceed further is to enter the realms of idle speculation; suffice it to say that Priestley's breadth of vision allowed him to create pictures of sufficient diversity to enable us to understand the railway as a formidable mix of operational, engineering and architectural skills at a time when it truly echoed the heartbeat of the nation.

Opposite, above: A composition of Linby Colliery signal-box on the GNR. Henry notes that three competing lines ran northwards from Nottingham for some 20 or 30 miles sharing the same valley for much of the way. They were owned by the MR from Nottingham Midland to Mansfield and Worksop, the GNR from Nottingham London Road, via the suburban line, to Shirebrook, and the GCR whose main line ran from Nottingham Victoria to Chesterfield.

Opposite, below: Hucknall Town on the GNR looking south. In its later years, this station was used only by local passenger excursion trains, the line being maintained for collieries in the area such as Linby. The GNR stations included Netherfield, Thorneywood, Daybrook, Bulwell, Bestwood, Hucknall, Newstead, Sutton-in-Ashfield, Skegby, Pleasley and Shirebrook, most being closed to normal passenger traffic by the LNER.

Ashchurch on the MR's Bristol to Birmingham main line looking north. This station is now demolished, junctions and signal-box removed and replaced by a two-platform halt almost devoid of shelter. The junctions seen here are to Tewkesbury and Malvern (GW) on the left, while the line on the right rejoined the main line at Barnt Green, presently used as a commuter line from Birmingham to Redditch with through services from Lichfield. The BR Standard 5 seen in the main platform is at the head of a train for Bristol. It has just negotiated a flat crossing at right angles, which connected the two branch lines in the picture.

Weston-on-Trent station, 6¼ miles south-east of Derby, on the line to Castle Donnington, was maintained for use by goods trains and diverted non-stop passenger trains, hence the condition of the fencing on the left. Note, in the distance, Willington Power Station. Abandoned goods yards were becoming familiar nationwide at the time when this picture was taken, 15 April 1957.

The Highland Railway's Foulis station was remote in the extreme and was the next station beyond Dingwall on the Far North line. Trains to Wick and Thurso omitted to call here. Only the short workings to Tain or Invergordon or Helmsdale served Foulis. A picture dated 29.8.61.

The LNWR station at Blencow on 9 August 1965. This was strictly the Cockermouth, Keswick & Penrith Railway. The NER had an interest in it to enable their mineral trains to connect the industries of west Cumberland and County Durham. The signal-box seems to be of Furness Railway design, hence the position of the nameplate.

Henstridge on the S&DJR lay 38 miles south of Bath MR station. A delightful rural scene and one of H.B.P.'s favourite pictures. Note the point rodding to interlock the crossing gates. The picture is dated 19.8.62.

The finials on the station nameboard indicate the location of this picture to be the Highland Railway, possibly Brodie, west of Forres and 22 miles from Inverness. Taken on 28 August 1961, the beauty of this tranquil station scene is much enhanced by the tablet apparatus located proud of the platform end.

Opposite, above: The Highland Railway station at Beauly was located on the Far North line between Inverness and Dingwall. At Beauly, the line turns from west to north to follow the adjacent Firth. Note that the main station building boasts the usual Scottish stepped gables. The date is 29 August 1961.

Opposite, below: The delightful MR station at Ullesthorpe on the Rugby to Leicester line was originally part of the Midland main line between Derby and London, Euston. It was later superseded by the Leicester to Bedford extension (for Hitchin and King's Cross) and finally by the Bedford to St Pancras extension, giving the MR its own line from Derby to London. Today, nothing exists of this scene, taken on 22 August 1959, apart from the road overbridge in the background, and the contemporary view from this point is into thick woodland with large trees growing where the tracks once stood. Ullesthorpe, only 3 miles by road from Lutterworth, was the last station on the Leicester to Rugby line and the run from there into Rugby was downhill and I have happy memories of Fowler 2–6–4Ts reaching speeds of up to 70 mph before slowing down over the huge blue-brick viaduct which connects this historic route with the LNWR main line.

The LNWR's Marston Gate station was located on an early branch of the London & Birmingham Railway. Running from Cheddington to Aylesbury it gave that town its first railway. When Henry first rode this branch in 1948, it was worked by a G2 class 0–8–0 goods locomotive hauling two composite bogie carriages and running tender first in one direction. He revisited the branch to make this picture on 25.5.61.

Old Dalby was located on a turn-of-the-century cut-off route which formed part of the Midland Railway's main line linking Nottingham with Glendon Junction, Kettering via Melton Mowbray and Corby. This route put Nottingham on a through line to the North and the Midland Railway's expresses were arranged as under:

     1) St Pancras via Nottingham to Carlisle
     2) St Pancras via Leicester to Manchester
     3) Bristol via Derby to Leeds

  Since closure, the bridge over the Trent into Nottingham has been converted to a road – the double-line railway making a one-way road. Railway conversion buffs please note! The remainder of the section as far as Melton Mowbray now forms the Old Dalby test track as mentioned previously.

The GWR's Cheltenham Spa station looking towards the buffer stops on 20 May 1964. It was formerly named Cheltenham St James, to distinguish it from Malvern Road, the main line station for Birmingham to Bristol trains. When Malvern Road was closed, St James became Cheltenham Spa while throughout, the MR station was known simply as Cheltenham and, locally, as 'Lansdown'.

Opposite, above: Oldham Central on the L&YR looking north-east on 14.4.55. At this time, the station was situated between Werneth and Mumps stations but is now dismantled. Approaching in the distance is Newton Heath-based Fairburn 2–6–4T No. 42287 at the head of a Rochdale to Manchester Victoria train.

Opposite, below: A typical Midland scene, complete with an MR milepost, at Butterley looking east on 29.8.55. This station was on a short double line linking the main lines at Pye Bridge and Ambergate and was used by excursion trains. It survives today, under preservation, as part of the Midland Railway Centre.

This is one of the pictures which has become detached from its notes and, despite considerable thought, Henry has been unable to identify it but suggests it may be on the Settle to Carlisle line; certainly the signal-box and signals are of Midland Railway origin, also witness the hills to the rear. The infrastructure details are magnificent but a reduction has already begun as the piles of sleepers indicate that the track to the left, which would have fed an island platform, has been lifted. Doubtless this picture's publication will ultimately reveal its identity.

6.   Priestley's People

People were the railway's *reason d'être*; it was created and operated solely by, and for the benefit of, mankind. It is therefore curious that a school of thought has become prevalent among the growing ranks of railway photographers that the best pictures of the railway are those unhampered by the presence of human beings. Obviously, a person or persons clumsily standing in the wrong place can, quite literally, ruin the picture but the fashion goes far deeper than this by doubting the very relevance of people at all.

From his earliest days as a photographer in the 1920s, Priestley welcomed mankind into his pictures as it quite literally illustrated the fact that railways were about people; never more lovingly were they embraced than when they fell naturally into a scene. In some of his most dramatic pictures the figures have a presence as vivid as those in an expressionist painting. One is reminded of the work of Munch: a woman fleeing up a platform, desperate to catch a departing train; the head and shoulders of a weary, home-bound worker protruding into the lower quarter of a picture depicting a suburban train in a station; or, perhaps most magnificent of all, the depiction of the twin brothers at Mile End Road in June 1939. These twins both joined London Transport on leaving school and are seen in middle age – in identical uniforms – lining up the 'ploughs' ready to feed them under the trams entering the conduit section. Quite apart from the presence of the twins, who look like mirror images of each other, the trackwork, the tram, placed geometrically centre stage, the architecture and the road vehicles of the time, render this picture a masterpiece with a maturity which belies the fact that Priestley was only in his twenties when he took it.

Such pictures as these are social comments which positively heighten the grandeur of the main subject, be it train or tram. Figures in historic photographs mature with time; fashion and dress add perspective to the period in which the picture was taken to provide another element of interest which will be of increasing relevance to future generations.

Opposite, above: Glastonbury and Street was located on the former S&DJR branch from Wells to Bridgwater, 5½ miles from Wells and 14 miles from Bridgwater (S&DJ). Ex-MR 3F 0–6–0s were a characteristic aspect of the line and here No. 43216 is seen at the head of a passenger train as Ivatt 2–6–2T No. 41304 awaits the road.

Opposite, below: Former MR 4F class 0–6–0 No. 43937 was a Leicester engine of many years' standing. It was an erstwhile performer and was regularly used on holiday excursion trains as caught here in this view looking west at Saxby. This station was the access point from the MR to the M&GN Joint Railway from the East Midlands. Access from the south was via Peterborough, GNR.

On 31 August 1958 the SLS organised a railtour of branches in County Durham which had been closed to passenger traffic. The special is seen here at Lanchester, NER, headed by K1 class Mogul No. 62059. Lanchester was on a line through a colliery area from Durham to Blackhill, 8 miles from Durham and 6 miles from Blackhill. H.B.P. was a member of the Railway Correspondence and Travel Society (RCTS), who often joined forces with the SLS on days such as this.

Opposite, above: Henry liked to capture the atmosphere of railtours and, while he entered into the full spirit of the occasion, he had the ability to take a detached view and produce remarkably candid pictures of a kind one would expect from an outsider; a similar sense of detachment is found in Lowry's pictures. This railtour, organised by the Stephenson Locomotive Society (SLS) had, as its star performer, MR 0–4–4T No. 58087

Opposite, below: Acton Bridge, 173 miles north from Euston, is the station before the flying junction at Weaver which separates the lines to Carlisle and Liverpool. This was a two-track section and the line swinging away to the left, behind the Up main, was for CLC trains to Northwich. The occasion here was a railtour on 31 May 1958 during which 'Crab' No. 42939 and 'Jubilee' No. 45593 *Kolhapur* managed to occupy the Up and Down main lines as part of the activities. Henry never failed to capture the sense of occasion of these tours when vast numbers of enthusiasts swarmed over the station areas in a way which would be utterly unimaginable today. The enthusiasts contrast poignantly with the sparcity of passengers; indeed, Henry stated that he had never seen many passengers at Acton Bridge.

The sheer magic of train-spotting on a hot summer's day next to an excitingly busy main line is conveyed in this glorious picture – right down to the obligatory 'swig of pop'. Steam trains forged a million happy childhoods. The scene is Retford, GN, looking north, and the date – 18 August 1959 – was deep in the summer holidays. A passing V2 class 2–6–2 completes the scene. Retford is 138 miles north of King's Cross.

Hunts Cross station was on the CLC main line, 7 miles from Liverpool Central on the route to Manchester and Sheffield via Godley Junction. The passing train in this undated scene is headed by Stanier 2–6–4T No. 42469.

Opposite, above: The shortage of passengers at many country stations during the 1950s is fully evident in Henry Priestley's work, but this view shows that the Midland station at Bleasby was better patronised than many. Taken on 11 May 1957, the passing freight is headed by ex-LMS 4F 0–6–0 No. 44215, allocated to 16A, Nottingham. Bleasby is 11 miles from Nottingham on the line to Lincoln.

Opposite, below: Thorneywood station was on the GNR's Nottingham suburban line. After London Road, this line branched off at Netherfield and Colwick and continued, via Thorneywood, to Daybrook, where it met the line to Derby. The line never paid its way and was closed to passengers during the First World War. This picture was taken during a railtour on 16 June 1951 looking north, and features ex-GNR C12 class 4–4–2T No. 67363.

I can think of no other railway photographer who made torrential rain a distinct feature of his work, but to H.B.P. it was another exciting dimension to a scene, as in this view looking east at Highbridge on the S&DJ network, with ex-LMS 4F 0–6–0 No. 44557 on a Burnham train. Behind the camera was a flat crossing over the GWR main line from Bristol to Exeter. A few miles away was a second flat crossing at Dunball. At both sites, however, the GWR was the older established, and therefore their signalmen controlled the traffic.

Opposite, above: A Stroudley 'Terrier' on the Hayling Island branch of the former LB&SCR on 24 May 1961 at the head of the 2.57 to Havant. Note the diminutive engine's height against the more modern carriage. This branch from Havant imposed a severe weight restriction on account of Langstone Bridge (over the harbour of that name) which connected the island with the mainland.

Opposite, below: The GWR station at Wellington in Somerset looking north-east. A Taunton to Exeter train is seen entering the Down platform line with the two fast lines in the centre. This train will climb to Whiteball Summit on the line where, in the Up direction, *City of Truro* is reputed to have touched 102.4 mph in 1904. Notice that the station nameboard incorporates (SOM) to distinguish it from Wellington (Salop). The picture is dated 9 August 1960.

The former GER station at Ware looking east on 15.6.57 with N7 class 0–6–2T No. 69683, allocated to 30B, Hertford East, with the 1.50 train from Liverpool Street to Hertford. The single platform to Hertford includes two prams – traffic which was not allowed on local buses.

When the grey accountants declared steam-hauled trains as uneconomic no consideration was given to the fact that they were a source of healthy occupation for millions of youngsters, a fact indicated by this picture of Darlington station looking north from the south end of the Up main platform on 10 October 1953. Gresley A4 Pacific No. 60006 *Sir Ralph Wedgwood* heads the 'Northumbrian' alongside one of the lovely A8, 4–6–2Ts which were a Gresley rebuild of Raven's D class 4–4–4Ts.

Pateley Bridge looking north-east on 24 March 1951 with the 1.25, Saturdays only, autotrain from Harrogate, headed by ex-NER G5 class 0–4–4T No. 67253, which was allocated to 50D, Starbeck. This picture shows typical West Riding scenery and stone station house. Note the vintage pram, which makes the BR-liveried G5 look positively modern. The pram's wheels seem to be almost as large as the trailing wheels of the locomotive! At this date buses could not convey prams.

Retford Great Northern shed on 18 August 1959. This scene characteristically shows small boys racing across the shed yard in those heady pre-electronic media days when the greatest fascination for children was to be found either on the railway or the football pitch – or, for many boys, both.

This rare scene depicts Tytherington on the closed MR branch from Yate to Thornbury. The occasion was a railtour on 26 September 1959 and Henry believes that the two boys on the derelict station platform were taking a picture as they had never seen a train on the line before. The railtour went through to Thornbury, where Henry took more pictures, but it was one of those days when the weather was against him. However, in this scene the flat light has enhanced the realism of this candid masterpiece.

Opposite, above: Totton was located on the LSWR main line from London, Waterloo to Weymouth, 3½ miles beyond Southampton. Here, an Up Bournemouth train is seen behind unrebuilt Bullied Pacific No. 34043 *Combe Martin*.

Opposite, below: Evidence of decay is apparent at an unknown location on the former NER featuring a grubby ex-LNER V2 class 2–6–2 hauling a brakevan, presumably as part of a pick-up goods diagram. At least the railway retains right of way at the road crossing. The tawdry motor car's driver sits pensively, like a brooding figure in a Munch painting.

The days when shopping trips were done by train are unimaginable to those brought up in a world of motor cars and supermarkets. The location is Langwith looking north; as the ladies thread their way homeward, the Fairburn 2–6–4T pulls sharply away – these engines were successors to the ex-LT&S 4–4–2Ts. Notice how Henry Priestley has used the foreground shadows to provide additional information along with compositional balance.

7.   Modern Trains

Priestley's impartiality about what train appeared in his pictures enabled him to cover the early years of modernisation and show the new forms of motive power in the railways' original shell. By comparison with steam, pictures of the early years of modernisation are relatively rare; railway photographers *en masse* revolted against anything which would displace steam and they certainly did not photograph it. All hell would be let loose if an errant diesel or railcar should perchance creep into a steam picture! And yet, for Henry, this would greatly intensify a scene, adding an entirely new dimension. A perfect example of this is seen on page 115 where two totally different, equally potent forms of motive power are seen in sharp contrast with each other.

Today, the perspective has broadened but there still remains a deeply rooted 'steam or bust' philosophy, notwithstanding the amazing diversity of contemporary trains and the fact that never in their history have Britain's railways been more colourful.

Priestley welcomes this diversity and colour and has risen to the challenge by converting his photography from black and white to colour. It is interesting that, despite having lived and photographed during the 'Golden Age' of steam, Priestley should find equal interest and fascination in trains of today. In his own words he sees no distinction; both are fascinating and relevant to the pictures he makes. Most individuals with a passion for modern traction are from younger generations who do not remember steam – few of those who do respond as readily to modern forms of traction as Henry Priestley.

Opposite, above: The former LNWR's Whitehaven Bransty station looking north on 9 April 1957, with a Derby two-car DMU on a Carlisle train. The line in the foreground leads to the harbour. The Furness line, through the tunnel to Corkickle and Barrow, is behind the buildings on the right. It joined the LNWR line north of the platform at which the DMU is standing. Notice the colliery in the background, so characteristic of the area.

Opposite, below: A fascinating view which is a reminder that in pre-preservation times, the Severn Valley Line was not all steam. The scene is Hampton Loade on 22 August 1961 and the train, the 2.05 Kidderminster to Salop, is one of the Great Western Railway's diesel railcars of the 1930s – the precursors of today's DMUs. Though primarily for branch line and cross country service, these units fulfilled other fascinating tasks including two sandwiched together, with a restaurant car in between, on Birmingham to Cardiff turns – services which knocked half an hour from the timings of conventional trains.

Knaresborough, NER, looking east to the tunnel, with DMU No. 51223 departing on the 12.15 Harrogate to York on 17.7.59. The picturesque and well-known viaduct is behind the camera.

This startling composition underscores H.B.P.'s belief that the railway abounds in pictorial opportunities irrespective of the type of train. Notice how the camera has caught the DMU in the optimum position. The location is unknown except that the train is bound for Nottingham and Henry points out that the signal box is of GN origin as witnessed by the skylight; the chimney is a subsequent addition and, to Henry, quite ruinous to the original design.

It is said that a picture is worth a thousand words but, for me, many of the greatest pictures are those about which a thousand words could be written. This picture is clearly one of them; taken at the former MR Shirebrook station, looking south, in the heart of the Nottinghamshire coalfield. The date is 26 March 1964, a time when the former goods shed at Shirebrook had been requisitioned as an acting HQ of maintenance for the new diesel locomotives currently being built. The new Brush Type 4s are Nos D1540 in the shed and D1565 outside on running trials as ex-LMS Stanier 8F 2–8–0, No. 48219, passes on a Down mineral.

Opposite, above: The line north of Inverness was dieselized early and in this scene, on 29 August 1961, No. D5339 approaches Lentran with the 6.50 Helmsdale to Inverness, which has become a mixed train. Lentran was a former Highland Railway station located some 6 miles from Inverness.

Opposite, below: Achterneed station looking west on the former HR's 'Road to the Isles' (Dingwall to the Kyle of Lochalsh). The train is the 10.45 Kyle to Inverness, headed by No. D5322 on 29 August 1961, a time when these locomotives had just taken over all Kyle workings, both passenger and goods. Achterneed was the first station on the branch at 4¼ miles from Dingwall and 59 miles from Kyle of Lochalsh.

Firsby, on the GNR's East Lincs line from Peterborough to Grimsby, was best known as the junction for Skegness, although it was also the junction for the Wolds market town of Spilsby. Here, we see Immingham B1 No. 61390 with the 12.46 Grimsby to Peterborough semi-fast which also called at Boston and Spalding. The DMU, No. 50038, uses the north side of the adjacent triangle to reach Skegness. Through trains from King's Cross to Skegness used the southern side and avoided Firsby. The date is 11 July 1959.

8.   Priestley's Golden Mean

Some licence may be taken in presenting these pictures under the heading 'The Golden Mean' but these scenes excel in their visual proportions, balance and harmony, elements which are the essence of the golden mean. As Priestley toured the network he was confronted by an endless variety of scenes which needed to be recorded; most would fall naturally into reasonable shapes to make a picture, especially when all possible camera viewpoints were considered. But Priestley is a communicator blessed with an innate sense of balance and proportion and he was invariably able to intensify such scenes. He was often thwarted by the vagaries of light; he had a limited amount of time at most of the places he visited, and if the light was wrong directionally or the day heavily overcast, the results were obviously imperfect. But on the occasions when a perceived harmony of form was augmented by complementary light, Priestley locked on to it with all the directness of a laser to produce astonishingly beautiful images rich in tone, form and rhetorical detail. The pictures in this chapter fall into this category. One reads a Priestley picture as one reads a piece of well-written text, effortlessly following the flow of information and logical assertion which culminates in a succinct and clearly understood expression.

Priestley's pictures have the advantage of being taken at a time when the railway abounded with interest; it was a virile system, full of fascinating details. Today's bowdlerised railway is stripped to the bare essentials in much the same way as our countryside has been raped of its wild beauty by accountancy-led agribusiness.

There is another essential advantage which Priestley had; he was able to place himself in the best position. Many of his pictures are taken from viewpoints which would be impossible today without the accompaniment of a COSS (Co-Ordinator and Site Safety) and a lookout – at a daily cost of some £200! Even many of his station platform pictures would be difficult today as the 'job's worth' mentality of many railway operators would even forbid this without an attendant shoal of paperwork. Equally impossible would be the many views he took from the driver's cab of DMUs when he had been able to ride with the driver to cover sections of line quickly, efficiently and from refreshingly varied viewpoints.

Despite all these advantages of photographing railways over past decades, they do not alter the essential brilliance of Priestley's photography; they simply enhance it. His status as a master of the golden mean remains undiminished.

Opposite, above: Ex-GW 0–6–0PT No. 9776 waits with a 'Toad' brakevan for 0–6–0PT No. 3661 at the head of a Newport to Brecon passenger train to clear the section at Pentir-Rhiw by exchanging tokens. This station, on the former Brecon & Methyr Railway, was a block post and passing place, with an island platform on the steepest run on a British main line, where trains were lifted from Talybont-on-Usk to Torpantau – Henry's recollection was of some 8 miles of 1 in 40. The uphill run of point rodding leads to points controlling the loop and 'escape siding' which diverges into the mountainside in case of a breakaway.

Opposite, below: Another flawless composition with not a blade of grass out of place, emphasising the fact that, whenever the conditions allowed, H.B.P. achieved pictorial perfection. The location is Whissendine, between Melton Mowbray and Oakham on the Leicester to Peterborough line The signalman in the MR box watches Henry photographing a Stanier 8F 2–8–0 with a Down rake of mineral empties on 11 July 1964. In spite of the date the tightness of the telegraph wires suggests cold weather.

This powerful picture is one of Priestley's comparatively rare portrait shots. It shows Peak Forest station, 36 miles from Derby on the MR Manchester line, looking north. A train of limestone empties is seen on the main line with Stanier 8F No. 48605, which was an 8E, Brunswick engine. There was a heavy traffic of limestone as a basic chemical to Northwich, ICI. The local goods is being worked by Coalville-based 4F 0–6–0 No. 43950, whose driver has taken an opportunity for a brief siesta. The tip, which adds a final touch of magic to this scene, consists of waste from the limestone workings. The date is 2 August 1960 and on the same day Henry went to Millers Dale, where he took a picture of Willesden-based diesel-electric No. 10202 on a Liverpool to Nottingham passenger.

Boughton (pronounced Booton) was originally an LDECR station – latterly Great Central. It was located 20 miles from Chesterfield between Ollerton and Tuxford. During the Second World War it was the site of a large War Department establishment. The ex-Great Central 2–8–0, seen in this view looking east, was running through tender first and has been caught perfectly by the camera. Notice the delightful station garden.

Brock, on the former LNWR section of the West Coast main line, looking north. The four-track section from Euxton did not extend beyond Preston. Accordingly, stations like Brock could expect few stopping trains. Here, keeping things moving, is ex-WD 'Austerity' 2–8–0 No. 90681 at the head of a mixed goods on 6 April 1957. The diamond on the signal post tells drivers that the section is track-circuited, eliminating the need for Rule 55 procedure.

Darley Dale looking south-east showing the MR signal-box and gantry. However, the main signal arm, left, is ex-LNWR. Notice the camping coaches in the background; these were popular attractions at places of beauty throughout the country. Northwich-based, ex-LMS 4F, No. 44025 is in charge of the Down goods. On the same day, 15 August 1959, H.B.P. visited Matlock Bath and Millers Dale.

This wide-angle view of Wells-on-Sea vividly recalls the GER's Norfolk lines. On the left is J17 No. 65521, a South Lynn engine, on the 1.35 train to Heacham, with Norwich-based D16 No. 62953 on the right. Today, the railway in Wells is a distant memory but this scene on 31 May 1952 shows a vigorous system. Note the coal wagons being unloaded manually for local delivery with covered wagons behind, revealing considerable freight traffic.

This picture is one of Henry's finest and remains etched clear in his memory. The unforgettable day was 10 March 1956. It had been a night of sharp frost followed by a crystal clear morning which inspired him to go to New Basford on the Great Central main line. The oblique lighting provides almost visible movement to the steam and smoke as the 2–8–0 emerges from Carrington Tunnel throwing the raised semaphore into superb relief. This picture captures the spell and magical atmosphere of the railway and yet is so rich in detail that it can be read like a page of descriptive text. Note the GC post in the foreground; over thirty years out of date when the picture was taken.

A scene looking north-west from the MR's Darley Dale station, approximately 20 miles from Derby. LMS upper quadrant signals are seen on the left while the Up express is running under clear signals of MR type. In truth, this may not have been a passenger express, as the train is headed by a former WD 'Austerity' 2–8–0, a type never seen in passenger service and which is more likely to be a movement of empty stock. An Up mineral train, with a Stanier 8F 2–8–0 in charge, stands in the running refuge.

Henry Priestley points out that the difficulty here was to avoid the illusion of various verticals growing out of the locomotive's chimney. This was done by waiting until the locomotive was just on the move. The location is Cheadle Heath, at the western end of the MR's 'through line' from Chinley to Manchester Central (10 miles with no station after Bugsworth – later Buxworth). The locomotive is No. 42763 – a Nottingham, 16A engine – and one of George Hughes's delightful L&Y inspired Moguls known universally as 'Crabs'.

Heckington looking east with a typical GNR signal-box and somersault signal. The train is the 2.39 Skegness to Birmingham on 27 July 1963. It is worked by Ivatt 2–6–0 No. 43108 bearing a 40E, Langwith Junction shed-plate. The weather conditions were perfect and, on the same day, Henry visited Kirkby Laythorpe and Sleaford West.

Opposite, above: Buntingford was the terminus of a GER branch extending about 14 miles north from St Margarets, near Ware. The N7 class 0–6–2T has been detached from the train to pick up a van. This striking composition is full of information, with the loading gauge beautifully highlighting the station and acting as a superb balance to the locomotive. This pre-Nationalisation scene is dated 3 August 1947 and, on the same day, Henry visited Ware and Roydon.

Opposite, below: This is another of H.B.P.'s favourite pictures, and for reasons which hardly need explaining. The location is the L&Y station at Werneth, near Oldham. Originally, Oldham was connected to the main line by the 1-in-27 gradient shown here which, at that time, was the steepest gradient in the country worked by passenger trains. This was later by-passed by construction of the direct line to Manchester Victoria via Hollinwood. The locomotive shunting in the adjacent goods yard is ex-L&Y 0–6–0ST No. 51458, which was a Newton Heath engine when this picture was taken on 14 April 1955. Henry knows of no other photograph which depicts this historic gradient post.

Bere Alston with ex-LSWR M7 class 0–4–4T No. 30225 at the head of a local train to Plymouth on 15.8.60. At this time, the Callington branch was worked by an O2 class 0–4–4T. H.B.P. comments that SR nameboards were, regrettably, in concrete, however, the bold elements of this composition are riveted together in brief, a masterpiece.

9. Continental Studies

The VRB at Vitznau station connects the shore of Lake Lucerne with the summit of Rigi Mountain. The station is level and the incline (one of the steepest in Switzerland) visibly begins at the platform end. It is rack operated to the summit. Now EMU worked, much evidence remains of former locomotive use. First, on the right, is No. 7, a preserved vertical boiler engine; secondly, the double-track loop for the locomotive to run round the train is visible; and thirdly, the turntable for reversing the locomotives. H.B.P. says that when he first saw this line in 1928, the locomotives were already abandoned.

A superb scene from Switzerland, full of impact and information. It is on the Mount Pilatus system and shows a train approaching the summit. Note the double-sided toothed rack rail.

For me, this is the most exciting of all the pictures Henry took from a moving train. It shows Landwasser Viaduct on Switzerland's RhB metre gauge Chur to Arosa line. Interestingly, H.B.P. described this route as a tramway, which it is in the town of Chur. The safety record of Swiss mountain railways is unequalled. Some years ago, an accident caused an English newspaper to complain, only to discover that the line was in France!

Selzthal is an important junction on the Austrian State Railway (ÖBB) network in the south of the country. The superb beast which Henry shows here is a former KK Stb Austrian State Railway Class 429, 2–6–2, which is a superheated version of Gölsdorf's Class 329. Gölsdorf was one of the world's greatest locomotive stylists and, during his tenure of office as chief mechanical engineer of the Austrian State Railway, produced some fifty different designs of striking appearance and with a distinctive family lineage.

Århus Quay, Denmark, with dock shunter No. 597 on 28 July 1952. The engine is seen on street track outside a typical piece of Danish domestic architecture. Henry was in Denmark as a guest of the Århus Cathedral Grammar School headmaster and took with him a party of some forty pupils.

This unidentified shed scene is possibly Vienna Nord depot, which had a considerable allocation of these 93 class 2–8–2Ts. Although most of the class were fitted with Giesl chimneys, these two are among the few that were not. The 93s were one of the stalwarts of Austrian Railways' motive power and were employed on secondary services in many parts of the country for almost fifty years, tackling gradients of 1 in 40 with 200 tonne trains.

Symmetry personified; 2 o'clock precisely – two halves of the picture, two trains. Perhaps this precision was not intended, but I suspect it was, and it works superbly. The scene is Angers in 1960. This is a French fortified city west of Paris and the capital of Anjou Province. Unusually in France it was served by competing railways before the unification that produced SNCF. These were the Paris/Orleans Railway and the ETAT (formerly the Ouest). Note also the Autorail diesel unit on the right and the clock, not on the 24-hour system.

Le Touquet Aeroport on the French Nord Railway with the arrival of a through diesel coach from Paris Nord. These 'Birney' railcars were built to American patents specially for the 170-mile journey from Paris and special attention was given to comfort and luggage space. This picture has all the freshness of a new line, a new train and a new airport. H.B.P. remembers the journey to be particularly comfortable and an early precedent of using DMUs for long distance travel. This was also one of the very early rail and airport connections which have become so fashionable and necessary in recent years.

10.   Light Rail

In common with his railway work, Priestley's light rail pictures extended into Europe where, in many cases, he was not running the same race against time as he was in Britain, and many of the systems he covered continue in vigorous use to this day. Splendid as these continental systems are in reducing congestion and pollution and doing much to make the cities they serve more civilized places in which to live and visit, they pale by comparison with the tramways Britain once had. In 1927, Britain had 14,481 trams used by 233 operators serving hundreds of towns and cities with a total of 2,514 route miles of track.

It is no coincidence that Priestley concentrated the greatest part of his photographic output on trains and trams as they are irretrievably related – light rail and heavy rail form the ultimate, efficient integrated transport system in cities and densely populated urban areas. It was a winning combination ripped up and scrapped by governments either incapable of, or disinterested in, the long-term well-being of the nation. Priestley realised all too well what was going to happen; he followed the *Daily Mail*'s vitriolic campaign against trams and set down on film as much of the legacy as he could, bringing to his photographs the same inimitable characteristics of the 'permanent way' in service to the community – the stuff and essence of our everyday world and, to coin a phrase, capturing the 'way we were'. I would add that it is the way we still ought to be.

Opposite, above: Car No. 561 at Koningens Brog on Rotterdam's light rail system on 9 August 1954. The policeman has been alerted because he thought H.B.P. was photographing a bridge, which at that time was a sensitive defence feature. Henry convinced him that the tram was his subject. It was also the switch, linking plain and interlaced track nearly under the tram, but his command of sign language did not run to that.

Opposite, below: Berne Central tram station is adjacent to the main railway station, a convenient arrangement yet to be adopted widely in Britain. Another tram system (to Solothurn) has a terminus below the railway station, and a third, to Worb, has running powers.

Henry Priestley's use of rain is put to excellent effect in this wonderful composition from the cobbled streets of Brussels. The system is the SNCV and car No. 10479 negotiates a particularly tight curve at the Av. de Schent on 6 April 1956. The scissors crossing in the foreground enabled trams to negotiate a double-line T-junction in all three directions. The photograph was taken from the leg of the 'T'. Brussels, Vienna and Milan had, at this time, the most extensive standard gauge systems known to H.B.P. in Western Europe. In addition, Brussels had an extensive metre gauge system (the Vicinal), reaching from several city termini over an immense mileage into the countryside. Many city boulevards had four parallel tracks; two standard and two metre gauge.

A magnificent portrayal of light rail and how it can be so integrated in city environments, given the necessary will. This superb composition is of the Nord Zuid Hollandsche (NZH), which ran from Amsterdam Noord to Volendam and Purmerend. Monnikendam, where this picture was taken on 28 August 1955, and Edam, of cheese fame, were on the Volendam route.

Tram No. A9 on the NZH, metre gauge line from Amsterdam to Haarlem and Zandfoort on 22 August 1955. Perfect traffic segregation is illustrated here with the tram bridge, a pedestrian bridge and road bridge all over an inland waterway.

Index